Dr. Grace LaJoy Henderson

FINDING MOTHER AFTER FIVE DECADES

A Story of Hope

Inspirations by Grace LaJoy
Raymore, MO 64083

FINDING MOTHER AFTER FIVE DECADES: A STORY OF HOPE
Grace LaJoy Henderson

Disclaimer. I have tried to recreate events, locales and conversations from my memories of them. In order to maintain their anonymity in some instances I have changed the names of individuals and places. I may have changed some identifying characteristics and details such as physical properties, occupations and places of residence.

Due to the delicate subject of mental illness, all names are fictitious. I have taken great precaution to ensure my mother could not be located, while still sharing my real-life story.

Mission. Sharing my story to help increase awareness of mental illness.

Goal. Reducing stigma. Fostering connection. Inspiring hope.

FINDING MOTHER AFTER FIVE DECADES: A STORY OF HOPE
Copyright 2020. Grace LaJoy Henderson
Written by Grace LaJoy Henderson
Published by Inspirations by Grace LaJoy
Raymore, MO 64083

ISBN: 978-1-7341868-3-3

All rights reserved. No portion of this book may be reproduced, photocopied, stored or transmitted in any form except by prior written approval of the publisher.

Printed in the United States of America

Praises for Finding Mother After Five Decades

"The author's description of having hope and feeling it diminish was really powerful. Her struggles of hope and disappointment were incredibly well-depicted." ~**Phoebe Shanahan, MA in English Literature**

"I felt that this book covered a lot of ground and was extremely well-written." ~**Jacob Kelow, High School Counselor, Kansas City Public Schools**

"An honest and relatable story. I like that the author's wish to find her mother came true. This book contains a lot of good tips for people who may be searching for someone." ~**Arica Miller, LMSW, School Social Worker**

"Finding Mother after Five Decades exemplifies hope, perseverance, and victory. It is an inspiring story for others who may be contemplating this journey." ~**Dr. Mary E. McConnell, Educator, University of Missouri-Kansas City**

"While reading about the author's setbacks and emotions I knew, eventually, I would be enjoying an awesome ending." ~**Yolanda Irvin, Brookside Charter School, Kansas City, MO**

"Anyone who has experienced the abandonment of a parent will know that they are not alone. I like the breakdown of the author's search for her mother." ~**Ana Wells, Raymore, MO**

"The author had the desire to find her mother and she found her! I like that she kept searching even when she became very discouraged!" ~**Kristen Driskill, Belton, MO**

Praises continued →

"This book will benefit others who have had similar experiences. They may be encouraged to search and not give up." ~**Shari Sanders, Belton, MO**

"*Finding Mother after Five Decades* is awesome! It gives a lesson to never ever give up. The author was determined and she found her mother. This is an amazing story." ~**Zahra Batool, MA in Psychology, Pakistan**

FINDING MOTHER AFTER FIVE DECADES: A STORY OF HOPE
Grace LaJoy Henderson

DEDICATION

To "April" for answering a phone and confirming that my journey in searching for my mother had come to an end. I have finally found her.

To my brother "Jerome", the first person I called when I suspected I might have located Geneva. You did some footwork of your own and helped confirm that the person I had come across was indeed our mother.

ACKNOWLEDGEMENT

The *Finding Mother Series* is my own recollection of my siblings' and my reunion with our mother after forty-nine years. When referring to my father, mother and siblings, I use fictitious names, as this is *my* story to tell. Their accounts may be different, as they may have perceived things from a different angle.

ABOUT THE SERIES

The *Finding Mother Series* is a complex, touching opportunity for readers to see into the author's journey to find her mother after decades. This series would be ideal for students at a secondary level who are searching for insight about the emotional conflicts and battles one must face when someone they care about has a mental illness. The four books in the series are segmented to provide specific lenses to the overall process, with a number of opportunities available for opening discussions about mental illness from both the author's point of view and her mother's.
~Leslie Arambula, MA Creative Writing, English Teacher

FINDING MOTHER AFTER FIVE DECADES: A STORY OF HOPE
Grace LaJoy Henderson

A WORD FROM THE AUTHOR
ABOUT THE FINDING MOTHER SERIES

Stories like mine are common and there is a sincere need to establish dialogue concerning this issue.

When I asked my mother how she felt about me publishing our reunion story, she laughed and said, "I guess it will be alright." Then she laughed again. She seemed flattered. Therefore, I really want her to feel proud about the way I present my recollection of the story. I told her I would not be revealing her real name or location.

To protect my mother's privacy, I have not revealed the full name under which she was found. I would never have found her under the name listed in my original foster care storybook. I believe that my personal recollection of our reunion details will inspire you. I hope it will decrease the stigma of mental illness in order to promote helpful discussion about this subject.

Due to my own personal struggle with the stigma surrounding mental illness, initially, I was only going to share the positive details of finding and reuniting with my mother. I did not intend to share any of the parts that were embarrassing for me. However, when others heard my story of how I found my mother after five decades, they told me they felt inspired. Many had similar stories. Realizing my personal story was intriguing, and could be helpful to so many people, I am sharing it…all of it.

FINDING MOTHER AFTER FIVE DECADES: A STORY OF HOPE
Grace LaJoy Henderson

TABLE OF CONTENTS

FOREWORD – DR. THERESA TORRES, PROFESSOR OF SOCIOLOGY	9
PREFACE	10
INTRODUCTION	11
CHAPTER 1 - BEFORE MOTHER LEFT	13
CHAPTER 2 - AFTER MOTHER LEFT	19
CHAPTER 3 - THE SEARCH	25
CHAPTER 4 - THE SEARCH CONTINUES	35
CHAPTER 5 - STILL SEARCHING	45
CHAPTER 6 - LOSING HOPE, THEN FINDING A GLIMMER	53
CHAPTER 7 - I FOUND MY MOTHER!	61
DISCUSSION QUESTIONS	71
QUESTIONS TEACHERS CAN ASK	72
FURTHER DISCUSSION POINTS	73
FINDING MOTHER SERIES	75
ABOUT THE AUTHOR	79

FINDING MOTHER AFTER FIVE DECADES: A STORY OF HOPE
Grace LaJoy Henderson

FINDING MOTHER AFTER FIVE DECADES: A STORY OF HOPE
Grace LaJoy Henderson

FOREWORD

A powerful, gripping read! *Finding Mother After Five Decades* is the emotional journey of the author to locate her mother who abandoned her when she was only two years old. This book held my attention and kept me wanting to know why her mother left and where she went. As the author unraveled the impact of mental illness on her mother's life, I felt compassion for the author, her mother, and siblings. This captivating book left me eager to read the next book in the *Finding Mother Series*.

Reading this story also offers hope to people in search of their parents.

~ Dr. Theresa Torres, Professor of Sociology
University of Missouri–Kansas City

FINDING MOTHER AFTER FIVE DECADES: A STORY OF HOPE
Grace LaJoy Henderson

PREFACE

When I estimated that my mother would be close to eighty years old, I nearly gave up all hope that I might see her again. *In Finding Mother after Five Decades*, I share specific details about my tedious journey of searching unsuccessfully, giving up, then finally finding my mother after forty-nine years.

FINDING MOTHER AFTER FIVE DECADES: A STORY OF HOPE
Grace LaJoy Henderson

INTRODUCTION

When my mother left in 1969, I was two years old, and when I finally found her in 2018, I was fifty-one years old.

Forty-nine years, that is how long it took me to see her face again. However, I like to refer to the timing as five decades because it was so close to the fifty-year mark.

This worn out folder represents every effort, challenge, and failure I endured in my very long and tedious search for my long-lost mother until the final success of reuniting with her. In this folder are birth certificates, birth records, marriage record requests, private detective reports, letters I sent, social security information, and the list goes on.

I finally found my mother on March 2, 2018. Just over a year later, on July 1, 2019, I began sorting through these items, placing them in chronological order, so that I could eventually lay out for you every hardship and obstacle I had to overcome in order to hug my mother one more time.

My first recollection of my mother was when I was two. I was too little to realize fully what was going on, but I vividly remember the day she left my siblings and me in the care of our father.

FINDING MOTHER AFTER FIVE DECADES: A STORY OF HOPE
Grace LaJoy Henderson

Over the years, this lack of motherly care was something that was constantly on my mind. Whenever I had the chance, I tried to get as much information as I could from my father, the person who knew her better than anyone.

When I finally came of age, it took me thirty-three years to find the mother I was yearning for.

Even as I was filling this folder up, I never truly believed the day would come when I would actually see my mother again. Now, it feels amazing to be telling the world how I have finally found her when, more than once, my hopes were crushed and I thought it would never happen for me.

Chapter 1

BEFORE MOTHER LEFT

She has to be somewhere! That is what I used to exclaim, frustrated when my mother seemed to have vanished into thin air and all of my search efforts were coming up null.

Why did she have to leave?

Why *my* mother?

Why do I have to endure such a devastating heartache?

Most importantly, why can't I find her?

Those were the thoughts and questions that lingered in my mind over the years, as the trail of my mother's whereabouts was getting colder with each passing day.

Even though I was only two years old when she left in 1969, I can recall with vivid details of numerous events that took place at that time.

One of the most heartbreaking memories I have is this one: My mother picking me up in her arms and walking out of the back door of our rental house. She walked, across the very tall, uncut grass to the back area of the lawn, lay face down in the grass and cried her heart out. I lay beside her and cried with her. At the time,

FINDING MOTHER AFTER FIVE DECADES: A STORY OF HOPE
Grace LaJoy Henderson

I did not understand why she was so miserable that she would sob so heavily in front of her little girl.

I only remember feeling heartbroken for her.

I felt her pain so very deeply.

It was like her pain was my pain and I hurt terribly for her that day.

I later learned that my father had called the authorities to have her picked up and taken, against her will, to a mental hospital.

So, during that moment of weeping in the grass, she knew she was about to be separated from her family.

It seemed as though my father had been insensitive to his wife's illness. But, I guess if she was posing a threat to herself and others, my father may have felt he was doing something good.

Here is a less heartbreaking, yet deeply hurtful, memory: I was in the car with my family, when my father and mother began to argue. I was no more than one or two years old, but I remember feeling like my father's voice was loud and abusive and my mother was quiet and hurt from the dispute.

It felt like the argument was not fair because my father was louder, stronger, and angrier, while my mother seemed weak and unable to defend herself.

During this particular quarrel, my mother took me in her arms, got out of the car, slammed the door, and walked away with me. I do not remember if my father had demanded her to get out or if it was her choice. I only remember her getting out of the car.

While I do not recall anything that happened after that, my oldest sister, Carla often expressed her surprise about how my mother and I made it home before *they* did even though they were in the car and my mother had left walking.

When I really look back, my time with my mother was a painful one. Although I have always remembered both good and bad, the bad was ugly. I heard stories about my mother's mental illness causing her to experience episodes, which resulted in her harming my siblings and me. Overall, my father and mother had a strained relationship. They both endured an enormous amount of pain, resulting in the breakup of our family.

Growing up, I blamed my father for my mother's emotional state. I felt like his physical abuse caused her to leave us.

Over the years, my brother Jerome tried to explain to me that our mother really *did* have a serious mental illness and our father was not to blame for that.

"You don't understand, Grace. Our mother was not the sane person you think she was," Jerome used to say.

He remembered it better than *I* did because he was the oldest of the six children and I was the baby. He explained to me

FINDING MOTHER AFTER FIVE DECADES: A STORY OF HOPE
Grace LaJoy Henderson

that my father usually physically harmed her because she physically harmed us.

Although I continued to blame my father, I *do* recall an instance where I know it to be true. My father came home from work one evening to find bruises on me. Mother had beaten me with a broomstick. In turn, he gave her a beating with the same broomstick. Not understanding the concept of revenge, I felt a deep sadness for the lady who gave birth to me. This is the only time I remember my mother hurting me, but not the only time I witnessed my father hitting her.

I never believed that my poor mother deserved to be abused regardless of the circumstances.

Right or wrong, that was just how I felt whenever I would think back about my parents' relationship. I guess my father was trying to protect us the only way he knew at the time. But, the way he went about it was very wrong in my eyes.

She was not mentally able to care for a family of eight.

My grandmother stepped in to help when she could, but I believe this still caused a major hardship for my father; they had six children, and he was carrying the entire family financially without any support from his wife.

I believe my father experienced a lot of stress and disappointment due to my mother having a mental illness and not being able to provide him with the support he desired from a wife.

FINDING MOTHER AFTER FIVE DECADES: A STORY OF HOPE
Grace LaJoy Henderson

She was unable to work, cook meals, or clean the house the way my father expected her to.

Then, to come home after a very long, tedious work day and find no dinner ready, the house dirty, or her having harmed one of the children, was an even heavier burden.

I imagine this had to be difficult for both of my parents as they were living in an era where the wife was naturally expected to perform the duties of the household while the husband worked.

FINDING MOTHER AFTER FIVE DECADES: A STORY OF HOPE
Grace LaJoy Henderson

Chapter 2

AFTER MOTHER LEFT

After my mother left, my father seemed very angry with her for not fulfilling his expectations. I do not believe he truly understood that she was not capable of being the person he needed her to be.

I believe he sincerely felt like he could just "knock some sense into her" and he tried his hardest so many times to do just that…unsuccessfully.

But, it is weird because even with all of the dysfunction, after my mother had left, my father would tell us how she could be the sweetest, most caring person in one moment, but then she would turn and be the total opposite in the next. He would say, "When she was nice, she was *very* nice, but when she was mean, she was *very* mean."

My grandmother often told me how smart my mother was and what a gifted pianist she was.

Whenever I heard people recounting all of these nice things about my mother, I wished she had stayed. However, when I think about her struggles, I feel grateful that she left to get the break she needed.

FINDING MOTHER AFTER FIVE DECADES: A STORY OF HOPE
Grace LaJoy Henderson

My father would often make statements that gave me clues about how he felt about her and her leaving. I did not like or agree with most of what he said. Since I blamed him for her absence, it was hard for me to understand his fury. I felt he was just making excuses.

Here are the statements he would make and how I felt whenever he would say each of them:

"I had to knock some sense into her." Whenever he said this, I would feel sad and did not believe him. I felt like he was just offering a dumb justification for hurting my mother. Even at my young age, I felt there was no excuse for him to have ever put his hands on her in anger.

"Your mother left, she doesn't want you." Both my father and maternal grandmother sat me down and told me this. My initial response was, "Well, if she don't want me, I don't want her *needer*." Grandmother thought my reaction was cute. I always felt like it was horrible for them to tell me my mother did not want me. As I grew older and thought about the issue, a part of me believed she wanted me. I felt they were just telling me she did not because they resented her for leaving.

I often thought, "What mother doesn't want a sweet little girl like me?" I felt like she ought to love and want me. I felt like she was just unable to care for me. That one comment, "she doesn't want you" was a big precursor to my feelings of rejection

FINDING MOTHER AFTER FIVE DECADES: A STORY OF HOPE
Grace LaJoy Henderson

and insecurity throughout my entire life. However, I have always felt grateful that she did not take me with her when she left.

Being only two years old, and the baby of my six siblings, I often imagined that she could have easily picked me up and taken me with her. Had she done that, I believe I would have ended up separated from her. That is what happened to all of the children she had after she left us. In that case, I would never have known any of my siblings.

"She never did anything for you all." As a little girl, I felt like it was my mother's mental illness that made her incapable of doing anything for us. I felt like my father did not understand that. I could feel his pain whenever he would say it, but unfortunately, she just was not able to help him care for us. In reality, *she* needed someone to take care of *her*.

"She did not want children, but didn't believe in birth control or abortion either. When she finally got some birth control pills, she would forget to take them." My mother had six children by the age of thirty and I believe this overwhelmed her. I have always understood her not wanting a lot of children, not believing in abortion, yet not believing in birth control. That was a lot of pressure for her to have to deal with. It seemed the full responsibility was on her as the woman.

When my father would talk about it, I felt he was not taking any of the responsibility and placing all the blame on her. I think my father may have been feeling a lot of guilt for continuing to get her pregnant. I guess back then, men could not do much when it came to birth control. It was the total responsibility of the woman. I believe my mother's mental illness made the situation even more difficult.

He mocked her voice as he reminisced about the way she used to say, "One of these days I'm going to go far, far away." Whenever my father altered his voice to mimic hers, I felt like he did not take her seriously and he should have. She obviously really felt that way because she actually *did* go far, far, away when she got the chance. However, he did not believe her at the time. I believe he thought those words were spoken out of her frustration.

He mimicked her as he recalled how she said, "I'm in love with Calvin" just before she ran away. Calvin was a patient in the mental hospital she was in at the time. People may have called my mother "crazy," but she had enough sense to leave an abusive relationship. So, when my father mimicked her about leaving with Calvin, I never blamed her for it. However, I would always wonder what Calvin's last name was. I wondered if she ever married him, if they stayed together after they had run away together, if they had any children together and if so, how many. So, hearing those words, "I'm in love with Calvin" brought

FINDING MOTHER AFTER FIVE DECADES: A STORY OF HOPE
Grace LaJoy Henderson

all types of questions to my mind…questions I strived to answer in my quest to find my mother.

"She couldn't keep a job." My father often complained about how my mother got a job working for a dry cleaner and was terminated when she refused to do things according to her boss's instructions.

He would say, "You can't do things *your* way when you are working for someone else. You have to do what *they* want you to do."

Whenever he complained about my mother not being able to keep a job, I felt bad for him because I knew he needed her to work to help pay bills. I felt badly for her because I knew she was not capable of holding down a job due to her illness. Thinking about the challenge of this situation causes me to feel sad, realizing this was unfortunate for both of them. I truly feel bad for what my father had to go through.

"If you all ever want to look for her, I will take you." Whenever my father would say this, I thought, "Of course I want to find my mother," and I felt like he should have just taken us to find her instead of saying that to us. But, then he would follow with, **"But, she may not receive you all."** I did not understand why my mother would not receive us. However, I believed him when he said it and those words made me feel afraid to tell my father I wanted him to take me to find her. So, as much as I missed her, and as bad as I wanted to see her again, I never asked my father if we could go and try to find her.

The thought of my own mother not receiving me made me feel a very deep hurt and I could not even begin to comprehend it.

The thoughts my father shared after my mother left were his truth. They were his reality, the way he experienced it, but I just refused to accept his side of the story because I did not know how things went down for her. Not knowing her side was one of my many motivations for spending an immeasurable amount of time over the years trying to find her. Now walk with me as I take you through the actual timeline of my search.

FINDING MOTHER AFTER FIVE DECADES: A STORY OF HOPE
Grace LaJoy Henderson

Chapter 3

THE SEARCH

I began missing my mother from the moment I was told she left in 1969. As a little girl, I desired to find her, bring her home and take care of her. I knew she was ill, and I always felt that wherever she was, she probably needed someone to love her. Unfortunately, I was too small to do anything. Besides my father had said she may not receive us even if we were able to find her. So, even though I missed her, it was just not in my heart to actually search for her back then.

I had already felt rejected by her leaving, I did not want to risk feeling rejected all over again if I were to find her.

As I discussed in my foster care storybook, *A Gifted Child in Foster Care*, in 1974, my father left town for work, leaving my siblings and me in a house alone. He promised to send money. He even and asked my grandmother, my aunt, and a lady who was his girlfriend, to come to the house and check on us from time to time. Somehow, unpaid bills left us with no electricity, no gas, and no water. A bare refrigerator left us hungry. A broken lock on the front door left us feeling afraid. The Sheriff removed us from the home and we became wards of the state.

FINDING MOTHER AFTER FIVE DECADES: A STORY OF HOPE
Grace LaJoy Henderson

When I was seven years old and living in foster care, my caseworker took me to visit my grandmother. During the visit, she told me about a call she had received from a hospital in another state, asking her if she could take a set of twin boys that my mother had just given birth to and left in the hospital. The hospital also told my grandmother that my mother had left a baby girl in that same hospital three years earlier and that the baby girl was adopted.

My grandmother told the hospital that she was too old to care for the twins. Hearing this made my heart ache. I was disappointed in her as I felt like she did not care what happened to the twin boys. I did not tell her I was upset because I was afraid she would think I was being disrespectful towards her.

The thing is that I wanted to know those babies because they were my siblings.

Even at my young age, I felt that my grandmother should have at least had the twins brought to Kansas City, Missouri so that I could get to know them. Since I was currently living in a foster home, I thought she could have had them placed in a foster home in Kansas City so that they would be close to us. I never understood why she chose to leave the twins in another state. At that point, I knew that I might never have another chance to know my baby siblings.

FINDING MOTHER AFTER FIVE DECADES: A STORY OF HOPE
Grace LaJoy Henderson

After learning I had more siblings, I never heard anything else about my mother. However, deep down in my soul I wanted to find her, see her, know her, touch her, talk to her, and shower her with all my love. However, the reality of my circumstances did not allow it. My young age limited me from being able to search for my mother.

As I grew older, I began to realize I actually had the ability to search for her. Becoming a mother at eighteen years old is what urged me to move things along. Having my own baby girl caused me to marvel at how a mother could just walk away from her beautiful little daughter.

Feeling this way caused me to make my first attempt to search for my mother in 1985. I walked down the street to the local Social Security Administration office and asked if they could help me locate my mother.

A woman explained their letter-forwarding program to me. She could not give me any information, but instructed me to write and submit an unsealed letter to my mother and leave it. If she was able to find contact information for my mother in their database, she would forward my letter and it would be up to her to respond. The lady said she would be unable to tell me if contact information was found.

I would never know whether or not the letter was sent unless my mother actually responded. I followed the instructions,

FINDING MOTHER AFTER FIVE DECADES: A STORY OF HOPE
Grace LaJoy Henderson

but never received a response from my mother. I did not know of anything else I could do at that time.

Ten years later, I came across a book that would teach me how to be my own private investigator. It provided guidance about how to locate hard-to-find people. With that paperback in hand, I began searching again.

November 14, 1995

I requested the marriage license, including the application, from the State Department of Public Health, for my mother and father but no record was found. I had sent a seventeen-dollar check for payment of the fee, and my check was sent back to me with along with my application and request letter. I was not sure how their marriage license would help me locate my mother, but I hoped the application would provide some hint that would possibly bring me closer to finding her.

I later visited a couple of Genealogical Research Libraries. Someone had told me that I might be able to find copies of marriage, birth, death, church, and school records there. There was an option to search very old census data to find records for ancestors, where they lived, their names and ages, and who their neighbors were. Through my search of the old census records, I learned that many families did not have cars back then. Therefore, it was not as convenient for them to move far away the way we

FINDING MOTHER AFTER FIVE DECADES: A STORY OF HOPE
Grace LaJoy Henderson

can today. As a result, many family members lived on the same block.

The Genealogical Research Libraries also had an option to search the Social Security Index by name or by putting in a social security number to determine if the owner of the number was still alive. I searched the Index to find my mother's social security number. I managed to find one for my father, uncle, grandfather and grandmother, but none for my mother, Geneva. Finding a social security number in the Index means the person is no longer living. As I could not locate my mother's, I concluded that she might still be alive, which heightened my hopes of finding her one day.

In addition to the Department of Public Health and the Social Security Index, during my search, I solicited information from resources such as: Bureau of Vital Records, Family History Center, and International Marriage Locator.

Online white pages were another helpful resource. I used it to search for addresses and phone numbers for my mother and the man who she ran away with, Calvin. I called one particular phone number for a Calvin with a Missouri address.

I chose to contact this particular listing because my mother and Calvin had run away from a mental institution in Missouri. So, I supposed Calvin may have possibly moved back to the state. When we spoke, he was very cooperative and told me he did not know Geneva and that he had no family in the area that we suspected my mother ran away to. After our conversation, I was convinced he was not the Calvin I was looking for. The main reason was because his voice sounded Caucasian and I believed the man my mother ran away with was African American.

March 28, 1996

I contacted an online people locator service, and they sent me a letter including information outlining how they are able to help people, like myself, find their lost loved ones. They gave two options. The first option was that they could provide me with the techniques to do the search myself. The results of my self-search would be sent to me in the mail. The second option was that they could actually perform the search for me. The latter would cost a whole lot more, however.

Their promise to me was that if I was unable to find my mother using the techniques they provided for option one, then, they would credit one hundred percent of my payment towards the cost of a full search that they would do for option two.

I did not end up using option two because I didn't have any reason to believe that their techniques would result in my finding anything more than what I had already found using the names I had for my mother.

That day, I searched for my mother's first and last name. I have a letter that they mailed to me informing me they were unable

FINDING MOTHER AFTER FIVE DECADES: A STORY OF HOPE
Grace LaJoy Henderson

to find any information about my mother after searching their nationwide database. It was almost two years later before I invested in another online people locator service.

January 9, 1998

I miraculously obtained a social security number that was supposed to be for my mother. I also learned the current last name my mother was using. Both of these pieces of information were surprise findings. I had been searching for her under her maiden name and the last name she had acquired from marrying my father. My heart was filled with excitement. I could not wait to search for my mother using her social security number and new last name. I had often been told that I could find my mother easily if only I had her social security number.

Finally, I had the key to unlock the mystery of my mother's location!

When I searched, nothing came up under that social security number or the new last name. I proceeded to search another online people locator service and contacted some people who I felt could possibly know my mother or in some way be related to her. Some shared her last name and some did not.

When that was not productive, I did a name search in an online phone directory. I also used it to conduct an online search for addresses and phone numbers for Geneva using the current last name I had just found out.

FINDING MOTHER AFTER FIVE DECADES: A STORY OF HOPE
Grace LaJoy Henderson

My father had already told me my mother ran away with a man named Calvin. Now that I had her current last name, I presumed that the man named Calvin might have had that same last name. The online phone directory had no listing for a Geneva with that last name and one listing for a Calvin. But, it was not the Calvin I was looking for.

My excitement about finding my mother with this new information was dwindling.

January 27, 1998

I searched again. This time, I ignored their last names because a private investigator had told me that a woman who is lost may have changed her last name due to marriage and so it could be harder to find her.

I sent a letter to four women named Geneva who shared her middle initial and date of birth. I informed the women that I had found their information through an online people search. The letter included my age and the names of my brothers and sisters.

I wrote, "I am searching for my mother who left my siblings and me when I was two years old[…]Please call me when you receive this letter to let me know if you are, or even if you are *not*, the Geneva that I am looking for." I invited them to call me collect, meaning I would pay for the long-distance phone call. Since this was in 1998, landline phones were still widely used and cellular phones had not become as popular as they are today.

FINDING MOTHER AFTER FIVE DECADES: A STORY OF HOPE
Grace LaJoy Henderson

I continued, "Or you can write me back using the self-addressed, stamped envelope that I have enclosed." I ended my letter by assuring them that my letter was for real and that this was a sincere search for my mother.

Well, all four of the women took my inquiry seriously because they each wrote me back to let me know they were not the Geneva I was looking for. One of them even followed up with a phone call to me! I felt happy to receive the responses, but, sad because my mother remained lost.

With declining enthusiasm, one day I sat down in a chair at my dining room table. I wrote a very long letter for my mother, beginning with, "Dear Geneva, my name is Grace, the youngest of the six children you left in Kansas City, Missouri back in 1969. Thoughts of you have lingered over the years and it is my dream to know where you are and how you are doing."

In my letter, I recalled how my father use to hit her and how, in my heart, he was to blame for her leaving. "He did his best to keep us together after you left," I penned.

"My deepest desire is to hear from you. I am not looking for a 'mother,' but would like to be there for you if you need anything." I shared with her the feelings of rejection I had experienced while growing up, due to her not being in my life. But I also told her that I have since triumphed over those feelings and that my life was good now.

FINDING MOTHER AFTER FIVE DECADES: A STORY OF HOPE
Grace LaJoy Henderson

After writing a few memories I had about her, I ended the letter by saying, "All my life, I have yearned to see you again, and I refuse to abandon hope that I will find you one day."

I poured my thoughts into this letter…

but I never sent it.

Chapter 4

THE SEARCH CONTINUES

January 10, 1998

I sent an inquiry letter to the Superior Court, Records Information Center, requesting any public information they could offer about my mother. I submitted her name, including her maiden and her newly discovered last name. I also provided her date and place of birth, her mother's and father's name. I gave the city and state where she was last known to be living, along with the information about the three children I heard she had.

I let them know I was Geneva's daughter whom she had left in Kansas City when I was two years old and that I was searching for her.

I concluded my letter by specifically asking for any birth, marriage, divorce, and death records that were public record. In response to my letter, they sent me a brochure about "How to Obtain a Copy of a Superior Court Document," which let me know the various documents that were available, the costs, and an official request form for me to fill out and send back.

Two days later, I returned to one of the online people locator services to look for the name Geneva, since I had no luck

FINDING MOTHER AFTER FIVE DECADES: A STORY OF HOPE
Grace LaJoy Henderson

with the social security number. None of the women named Geneva, with her current last name, shared my mother's date of birth. Therefore, they sent me a list of fourteen women named Geneva who did not share her last name, but who shared her date of birth. They indicated that if my mother had a last name change then one of the women named Geneva listed on the report could be her.

This search did not include phone numbers, and since none of them shared my mother's middle initial, I did not bother to reach out to any of them since I had already written letters to four women named Geneva from a prior search list, who actually shared her middle initial.

Three days after that, I received my own birth records from the medical center I was born in. I had ordered them on January 2, 1998. The records showed the names of the doctor who had delivered me. They showed my birth weight and height, and the exact time I was born. They even showed my temperature, pulse, blood pressure, weight, how much milk I drank, and even the level of pee and poop in each diaper daily for the entire five days I was in the hospital.

My birth records also listed my first name as "Girl" for the first couple of days after I was born. By the fourth day, it listed my name as "Grace." I presume I was finally given a name after about two or three days of my birth. I also noticed the middle name "LaJoy" was present on the discharge paperwork.

I had always known that was my middle name. I just felt surprised to see that someone had given it to me at the last minute.

Because of my beautiful and unique first and middle name, throughout my search, I always imaged that if my mother ever heard my name, she would immediately know I was the baby daughter she left so many years ago.

I was released from the hospital in excellent health.

My birth records showed that my father took me home from the hospital. They also indicated that my mother was a patient in a "state hospital" at the time of my birth. The full details were unclear. The discharge paperwork, that was supposed to be signed by my mother, was signed by my father.

In addition to my father's signature, the discharge papers included my infant left and right footprints and my mother's right index fingerprint. My father's signature served as certification that he compared the Ident-A-Band, affixed on me, with the identifying information in my record. It also served as certification that he had examined me and determined that he was taking home the right child.

After reviewing my birth records, it occurred to me that maybe my mother was unable to take me home because she was in a mental hospital.

FINDING MOTHER AFTER FIVE DECADES: A STORY OF HOPE
Grace LaJoy Henderson

I presumed that the "state hospital" referred to in my birth records was actually a "mental hospital." It also occurred to me this might be the same thing that happened to the three babies that she had left in the hospital back in the early 1970s.

I presumed that she did not necessarily "leave" those children in the hospital, but was unable to take them home due to being in a mental hospital at the time of their births, causing the babies to become automatic wards of the state.

I was lucky enough to have a father who was able to take me home from the hospital when my mother could not.

January 20, 1998

I learned that one of the digits in the social security number I had received for my mother was incorrect and then I was given the correct number. With the right social security number, I searched online again. I still did not locate my mother. But, this time, I found a 1997 record for a person named Kevin connected with her social security number. The record showed a middle initial, last name, mailing address, phone number and a birth year of 1975.

I called the phone number and learned it was a college dorm. No one by the name of Kevin was living there. I felt like I had hit yet another dead end.

I thought it was weird that I was not able to find any trace of my mother with her social security number.

FINDING MOTHER AFTER FIVE DECADES: A STORY OF HOPE
Grace LaJoy Henderson

I also thought it was strange for my mother's social security number to be connected with someone who was born in 1975, especially since she was born in the 1930s.

I wondered if Kevin could be my sibling.

I conducted additional research on his full name, but I was unable to find a matching name anywhere.

Now that I had what I believed to a be a good social security number for my mother, I sent a letter to a federal government agency's Office of Disclosure requesting to locate my mother as a missing person. I included my mother's name, date of birth, her parent's names, her place of birth, and her last known address. I do not remember if I ever received a response from the agency. Obviously, I did not locate her as a result.

January 21, 1998

The last online people locator service I used was never actually able to find any women named Geneva who shared her current last name *and* date of birth. So, I requested a report for a list of women named Geneva who shared her current last name, with *any* date of birth, and with phone numbers included. I received a list of four people with a letter stating that with the number listings they found, there was a high probability that I will locate my mother. I called all four but, to my dismay, none of them turned out to be the Geneva I was looking for.

FINDING MOTHER AFTER FIVE DECADES: A STORY OF HOPE
Grace LaJoy Henderson

By this time, I had used the online people locator service to conduct several "Geneva" searches using all the last names I had for her; I even searched with no last name. I used it to search for Calvin and for my mother's social security number, all with no success.

Since I was unable to find my mother using her social security number, it increased my suspicion that she was locked away in a mental hospital. I had always heard she was in and out of mental hospitals before she had left our family. She had run away from one of them with Calvin, never to return. After she left, I had heard she had abandoned at least three newborn babies in a hospital in another state. So, my thought had always been that she was in a mental hospital somewhere in a different state.

April 27, 1998

I searched online business pages. I called and wrote letters to several state and county departments of mental health service agencies, asking if they could tell me if my mother was currently, or if she had ever been, a patient in any of their facilities. Many of my phone calls resulted in either "she is not a patient here" or a referral to other possible mental health institutions in the area.

Within three weeks, I received a written response from two of the agencies. A State Department of Human Services informed me in writing that they have no record of my mother being a mental health patient. A County Department of Health and Human

FINDING MOTHER AFTER FIVE DECADES: A STORY OF HOPE
Grace LaJoy Henderson

Services, informed me in writing that, after a meticulous search with a combination of all possible last names, they found that my mother had never been admitted in their psychiatric hospital. The letter also stated they were going to submit my inquiry to another institution so they may search for her, too. I noticed both response letters were from each institution's Medical Records Administrator.

May 4, 1998

I received a copy of my mother's birth certificate from State Department of Health. To my surprise, it was a "Delayed" birth certificate, listing my grandmother as my mother's "birth" mother and my grandmother's husband (who was actually my mother's blood great uncle) as her birth father.

I had always known that my grandmother adopted my mother when she was two years old. I also knew she changed my mother's name, her birthplace, and changed her birth month, retaining the correct year of birth.

As you may have figured out, my mother's adoptive mother was actually my mother's aunt through marriage. A bit perplexing, I know.

The birth certificate did not appear to be a normal adoption, which left me wondering just exactly how my grandmother got my mother. My grandmother would often tell me the story of how she adopted my mother:

FINDING MOTHER AFTER FIVE DECADES: A STORY OF HOPE
Grace LaJoy Henderson

She would recollect, "My husband, Joe, and I went out of town to visit his family. While there, we met his great niece, two-year old Ginny. She was living with her mother, Joe's mentally ill niece. She had given birth to seven children and had lost legal custody of them all except her youngest, Ginny. When I tried to give her advice about how to take care of Ginny, she became aggravated and told me to 'take her.' So, I did."

Grandmother took Ginny home with her and changed her name to Geneva. Knowing that story, I was surprised to see Grandmother listed as *birth mother* on Geneva's birth certificate.

The next day, I sent a request and a blank check, with a note "not to exceed twenty dollars," to the Clerk of Superior Court. I asked them to search for a possible divorce record for my mother, Geneva and my father, Jerome between the years of 1967 and 1975. I sent an identical request asking them to search for a possible marriage record for my mother, Geneva, and Calvin between the years of 1975 and 1998.

Within one week, I received a response for both stating no record was found. They both sent my blank check back to me since they did not find the record I requested.

July 8, 1998

In search for more answers, I wrote a letter to the Department of Health and Human Services, Vital Statistics requesting marriage records for Geneva and Calvin during the years of 1968 through 1975. I received a certified statement of no record on file. I also requested divorce records for Geneva and my father during those same years; just in case my mother had filed for a divorce after leaving Kansas City.

After all of those attempts, Mother was still missing. Fatigue overpowered me. I felt like all avenues had been exhausted. It seemed Geneva would never be found, so I took a break from searching and just enjoyed my life.

It was during that break that I published my first book of poetry, began conducting workshops for aspiring authors, and earned my Doctorate degree.

September 11, 2008

My brother gave me a copy of my father and mother's divorce order dated 1971. He had held it for years, but I had not known he had it.

In the past, I had been searching in the state I heard my mother had moved to. Since she was the one who left, I was thinking she was the one who had filed. I had actually forgotten how my father filed on his own in Kansas City.

I was around five years old at the time of their divorce. I actually remember my father talking about his intentions and efforts to divorce my mother because she had abandoned us, and he did not know where to find her to get her signature for the divorce paperwork.

FINDING MOTHER AFTER FIVE DECADES: A STORY OF HOPE
Grace LaJoy Henderson

I also remember his relief the day the courts granted him the divorce and custody of us, his six children.

Because of what my father went through to ensure the court awarded him custody of us, I felt like my father truly wanted us. This gave me a sense of security, like no one would ever be able to take me away from my daddy.

Chapter 5

STILL SEARCHING

At one point during my search for my mother, I wanted to try to find some of her biological family. Since my mother had been adopted and had her name, date of birth, and birthplace changed, I did not know any of her blood relatives.

It was like my grandmother had erased any trace of my mother's whereabouts even before she ever left our family.

So, not only was it difficult to find my mother, it also seemed impossible to locate members of her birth family. I searched old census records, looking for Joe, my mother's great uncle who raised her along with my grandmother.

He was the only blood relative whose name I knew so I thought I would find him, which would then lead me to other family members who were connected to him. However, due to Joe having such a common first and last name, there were tons of them listed in the census records. As a result, it was impossible to tell which one of them was the correct one.

So, I gave up my attempt to locate my mother's blood relatives, and placed focus back on actually finding *her*.

FINDING MOTHER AFTER FIVE DECADES: A STORY OF HOPE
Grace LaJoy Henderson

I walked into a private investigator's office and asked if he could help find my mother.

When he learned I had her social security number, he said he could definitely find her. However, I would have to pay the required fee in advance. I informed him that I had searched my mother's social security number a few times and had not been successful in finding her. So, I was reluctant to pay a fee to learn something that I already knew.

Understanding my hesitation, the private investigator agreed to search first and then if he found anything more than what I had already found, I would be required to pay for the additional information. He searched and, just as I suspected, he was only able to find the person named Kevin connected with my mother's social security number, and nothing more. He was puzzled because he truly expected that he would be able to uncover more information with that number.

Once again, a search was conducted that did not lead to finding my mother.

I had a similar experience with a second investigator.

A third investigator tried to locate my mother at no charge as a favor to a young woman who wanted to be a blessing to me. Sherry was hosting a women's empowerment event, and wanted to find my mother and reunite us during the affair. It was her belief that the attendees would feel uplifted by my story.

FINDING MOTHER AFTER FIVE DECADES: A STORY OF HOPE
Grace LaJoy Henderson

She asked me to give her all the information I had of my mother. I cautioned her about the challenges I had experienced in my search even though I had her social security number.

She still seemed to have faith that her private investigator could find my mother, so I gave her the information and hoped for the best.

Leading up to the event, I felt like even if they did find my mother, I could not imagine her agreeing to a reunion in front of strangers. I doubted the investigator's ability to pull off the reunion. Nevertheless, I felt grateful for Sherry having the heart to want to try it.

Days before the event, she gave me the news that her investigators had been unable to find my mother. Since I had not really allowed my hopes to rise up, I did not feel let down. I still attended the event and had a lot of fun. After the event, I gave searching a rest for a while.

March 24, 2009

I had just finished writing a new book and was preparing a national press release to promote the paperback. It occurred to me to use that same announcement as an opportunity to try to locate Mom. So, I coupled information about the book and my missing mother in one write-up.

Geneva had been gone for forty years when I publicized that press release. She would have been around seventy-years old,

FINDING MOTHER AFTER FIVE DECADES: A STORY OF HOPE
Grace LaJoy Henderson

so I still had some hope of possibly finding her alive. After the press release was made public, I met a very helpful woman who had access to non-public resources that could help locate my mother.

She offered to help, asked me for all the information I had, and conducted a very thorough search for my mother. She found an address that she believed was my mother's. I used an online map to locate the address. I also searched online for the property report and found a possible owner for the property. It was interesting to find a potential landlord, but it was not helpful to my search.

I was not convinced my mother lived at this address, but I sent a letter to her there just in case.

I wrote, "My name is Grace. I am the youngest of the six children you gave birth to before you left Kansas City, Missouri in 1969. You were married to my father, Jerome, who is no longer alive." I continued, "Your other children and I are all doing very well and we have longed to see you again. I have searched for you for many years, but have not been successful in finding you."

I included my phone number and address and asked her to contact me. I even included a self-addressed, stamped envelope so she would not have to pay for postage if she chose to write me back.

I concluded, "There is a lot more I wanted to say, but I want to give you the opportunity to respond to my letter."

I never received a response and this fueled my doubt about that being her address.

April 2, 2009

The helpful woman's search revealed the same Kevin who I had located during an online search nine years ago. But, there was something special about the record she found. It listed a different middle initial, last name, and date of birth for Kevin. The record date was January 1997. I presumed this was the same record that I found for him back in January of 1998, but with a corrected name and date of birth.

I was thinking that Kevin could possibly be one of the children my mother had after leaving us, thus my half-brother.

I did additional research on the corrected name and found several family members for him. None of the phone calls led to any new information so I eventually gave up on that lead. However, I never stopped wondering why my mother's social security number was connected with Kevin.

The next day, I sent a note with pictures to my mother through the Social Security Administration's letter forwarding program. Since so many years had gone by, I thought I would try again. The rules were still the same. They would notify me if they did not find a Social Security Number for her. However, they would not be allowed to notify me if they found an address or were able to forward my inquiry.

One month after I left the letter, I received correspondence from the Social Security Administration office, which included the pictures I had enclosed.

They were not allowed to send pictures, but they did not return my note. This led me to believe that it had been sent. I never received a response, so I was not sure if my mother just never received it, or if she received it and chose not to respond. The latter was hard for me to accept. So, I just told myself she never received it because that was easier for me to comprehend.

September 30, 2009

I published my foster care story, and purposely included real names for my siblings and mother, with hopes someone would recognize the names and provide information that would lead to finding Geneva. It had been forty-one years since she had left.

December 16, 2009

A television show producer learned about my foster care story through an online search and offered to assist me in finding my mother in turn for me coming on the show for the reunion if her search was successful.

When the producer learned I had my mother's social security number, she said she felt very confident that their investigators would be able to find her. I told her of the past

FINDING MOTHER AFTER FIVE DECADES: A STORY OF HOPE
Grace LaJoy Henderson

challenges I had with searching her social security number, but she was hopeful that their show detectives would have more success.

The thought of the show finding my mother and me being able to give my siblings the good news caused me to become excited and accept her offer.

She provided me with a twelve-page application to fill out and return; requesting my name, children's names, occupation, and information about the person I was seeking.

That long list of questions included, *"How will finding your relative change your life?"* I answered, "It would satisfy my longing to see her, meet her, and to know how she is doing." And, *"If you saw her again, what is it you would like to say?"* My response was, "I love her. I have missed her. I do not blame her for leaving."

It inquired about my entertainment experience and medical history. I felt puzzled about why they wanted to know all of that. Nevertheless, I answered all of the questions.

The last request was for me to nominate someone else to be on the show. I responded, "It would be great if you could find my three half siblings, whom my mother gave birth to after she left. Also, my five siblings, who my mother left, would possibly want to come on the show if our mother is found."

FINDING MOTHER AFTER FIVE DECADES: A STORY OF HOPE
Grace LaJoy Henderson

Finally, the entire application was complete and submitted. Hopeful emotions ensued as I waited for a response.

A few weeks later, the producer called, apologizing that the show was unable to locate my mother.

In my heart, that outcome was somewhat expected based on my prior search experiences. Still, feelings of disappointment arose because I had been hoping that maybe *this* would be the moment that I would finally be able to reunite with my mother…but it was not.

By now, I had sent numerous inquiry letters, hired investigators, examined public records, and conducted online people searches. Victory was out of sight and hope was dim…

Chapter 6

LOSING HOPE, THEN FINDING A GLIMMER

There were times when I searched actively for my mother, like when I got a new idea or a possible lead. Then, there were times when I ceased to search. It was during those inactive times that I felt weak in my hope, like there was nothing more I could do. As if I was never going to find her.

It was during those times when I hated to mention my discouragement to people, because I knew they would attempt to help by giving me things I could try.

I used to run after every hint people told me to try but, when nothing ever worked, I became annoyed. I felt tired of people telling me "You should try this" and "You should try that" when I felt like I had tried *everything*.

Searching and not finding anything was disappointing, but the times in between my active searching were the most frustrating.

I used to enjoy watching talk show reunions. Those types of shows once brought me hope that I would one day be reunited

FINDING MOTHER AFTER FIVE DECADES: A STORY OF HOPE
Grace LaJoy Henderson

with my mother. However, after writing to several of the shows for help and receiving no reply, I became saddened. I began to feel insignificant, like my story was not important enough to be chosen. I understood that those types of shows received many requests and they could not help everybody.

But, still I could not help feeling slighted and overlooked.

As time passed, I realized my mother was getting older and older; the chances of finding her alive were becoming slimmer and slimmer.

These shows that once gave me hope, now caused me to become disheartened.

One day, I was watching a talk show. On this show, a twenty-two-year-old woman was granted a surprise reunion with her biological sisters and mother after over fifteen years. They were all thrilled to find each other, but I did not feel cheerful for them the way I once did when I would watch reunion shows.

My optimism was fading.

Instead of feeling hopeful, I was beginning to feel resentful. Instead of feeling happy for the families who were reunited, I was beginning to feel mad. Instead of feeling inspired by their good fortune, I was beginning to feel hateful and jealous.

Because of my increasingly raw feelings, I eventually stopped watching reunion shows altogether. I purposely avoided those types of shows because they revealed the harsh reality that

FINDING MOTHER AFTER FIVE DECADES: A STORY OF HOPE
Grace LaJoy Henderson

my mother was missing and I may never find her. I decided that if I could not find my mother, then I would try once again to locate her family members and maybe even try to find my siblings that I learned she had given birth to after she left.

October 31, 2013

I submitted my DNA to two online sites and began contacting DNA relatives that I felt could be kin to my mother. I located two female cousins who I thought favored my mother, and two male cousins. One of the males was a possible first cousin and looked just like my brother, and the other was a possible second cousin and had my mother's facial features. I spoke with each of them to see if we could determine a connection of exactly how we were related. The closest I got was learning that my first cousin's father was possibly my mother's biological brother, and that his grandfather was likely my mother's father.

It was a good feeling to find cousins related to my mother in some way, but I was still feeling hopeless about finding my mother.

December 17, 2017

I received a phone call from a longtime friend whose mother left her when she was two as well. She told me about a television reunion show, which specialized in cases like hers and mine, in which the person seems impossible to locate. She said this show had reached out to her with the hopes of finding her long

FINDING MOTHER AFTER FIVE DECADES: A STORY OF HOPE
Grace LaJoy Henderson

lost mother. In her excitement, she asked me if I was still looking for my mother.

I told her I had lost ALL hope and was not interested in even considering making any more efforts to find my mother. I told her I had done absolutely everything in my power to try to find that woman and had zero motivation to try anything else. However, I wished her much success in finding her mother.

Believing my mother was nowhere to be found, I continued searching for my siblings. While looking for them, I began thinking back about my friend's phone call. I realized her hope actually rubbed off on me enough to consider going online and watching the reunion show that she had received the phone call from. Even though reunion shows had made me feel unhappy in the past, I mustered up some courage and began watching some of the episodes.

While observing the excitement of people who found their long-lost family members, in particular their mother, I felt so very jealous of them.

I felt like their reactions of shock and happiness were fake. I just did not like those people because they had finally found their birth mothers, while my mother's whereabouts were still a mystery.

I just did not feel like finding my long-lost mother would ever become a reality the way theirs had.

FINDING MOTHER AFTER FIVE DECADES: A STORY OF HOPE
Grace LaJoy Henderson

As I continued watching episode after episode, I felt amazed while witnessing people finding loved ones who were over eighty years old, which was the age my mother would be.

A very slight glimmer of hope crept inside my heart all of a sudden.

I began to wonder if maybe it could be possible for me to find my mother. I found an application on the show's website, filled it out, called the show and intended to send it, but I never found the courage to actually do it. I was afraid of my hopes getting crushed once again.

In the meantime, I continued searching for siblings. I even located an investigator to try to find my siblings. It was rather difficult, however, because I had no idea what my siblings' names were. Furthermore, I did not know anyone who could give me even a clue of what their names might have been.

February 2, 2018,

I called a caseworker at the Department of Children and Families, asking if they could confirm whether my siblings were adopted through their agency.

I spoke with Elsie, who asked me for my mother's name and any information I had about when my siblings were born and what their names might have been.

I gave her approximate birth years based on what my grandmother told me back in 1974. I did not know their first

FINDING MOTHER AFTER FIVE DECADES: A STORY OF HOPE
Grace LaJoy Henderson

names, but I told her I believed their last names might be the same as the new last name I found for my mother. She told me she would research their databases and follow-up with me by email with the results of her search.

One week later, Elsie sent an email, advising me that I may be able to request a copy of my siblings' original birth certificates, not their adoptive birth certificates. About one hour after that, she sent the follow-up email that she had promised.

Her email stated she was not able to determine if my siblings were adopted through their agency based on the information I provided.

She told me that if I find out their exact names and dates of birth, to feel free to contact her and she would check the databases again with that information. At the end of her email, she provided some resources that she thought might help me in my search.

Among those resources were the Department of Health, a few online adoption databases and some online DNA testing and genealogical services.

I responded to her email thanking her for her help. I also provided her with the name and date of birth for Kevin, the young man who I had found connected to my mother's social security number, and asked if she could check her databases for him. I told her that I had always wondered if he could be one of the half-

FINDING MOTHER AFTER FIVE DECADES: A STORY OF HOPE
Grace LaJoy Henderson

siblings my mother gave birth to after she left. I told her I had done a lot of research on him, but never found anything.

Eleven days later, Elsie responded to my email letting me know she was unable to find any matches for Kevin. She also told me that their databases were not set up to search social security numbers, so she was unable to search to see if they had a case for my mother.

She again wished me luck in my search and told me that if I get more information in the future she would be happy to check their databases again.

I thanked her again for her help and told her I would be sure to reach out to her if I got more information. Even though her efforts had been unsuccessful, I felt grateful that Elsie was so nice and helpful to me.

I continued to watch episodes of the reunion show, endlessly imagining how I would feel if I were to miraculously find my mother; all along believing it was impossible and sensing it was best to only focus on finding the children she had after she left.

In the meantime, my big sister Carla had been missing for several years and was nowhere to be found. I am referring to the big sister I grew up with and lived with. Carla had been clean from drug use for over five years, when she moved away from Kansas

FINDING MOTHER AFTER FIVE DECADES: A STORY OF HOPE
Grace LaJoy Henderson

City. While living out of town, she reported that her life was going well. She was even providing counseling to other drug users.

The last time I saw her was when she had come to Kansas City for a visit. She looked beautiful, wearing a stylish red two-piece skirt suit, a shoulder-length wavy hairstyle, and evenly-applied makeup. We went to church together and ate dinner at a restaurant afterwards. She came to my house, where we talked and looked at pictures. Carla loved pictures!

After she returned to her home state, we talked on the phone a few times until suddenly her phone service was disconnected. My siblings and I lost contact with her for about four years. Finally, I located her daughter, my niece, and *she* did not know where her mother was!

Apparently, Carla had come upon some very hard times and did not feel like she could ask anyone for help. She became homeless at one point and eventually went missing. She was a great sister who had always been very kind and loving towards me. I feel sorry for the adverse turn of events in her life and I often wish I could have done something to keep it from happening.

It has been well over ten years since she had been lost. Every once in a while, I would do searches to try to locate her.

Chapter 7
I FOUND MY MOTHER!

March 2, 2018

On this day, I opened an account with an entirely different online people locator service in an attempt to find my oldest sister, Carla. I found some information about her, but was unable to locate her. I had five days of unlimited searches.

After I finished my search for my sister, I decided to perform one last search for my mother.

I did not really expect find her, but I felt somewhat hopeful that I might at least find some information about her. I definitely did not think I would find her alive. I searched and for the very first time in all of my years of searching, I received a hit for my mother's name, exact state, and date of birth! I even saw a current email address for her. I was thinking I had actually found current information for my mother and feeling like this could actually be the end of my very long journey.

However, I was scared to get happy too quickly.

In the past, I had been able to find numerous women with my mother's current first and last name, but none who shared both her state and date of birth. I had also been able to find those women

FINDING MOTHER AFTER FIVE DECADES: A STORY OF HOPE
Grace LaJoy Henderson

named Geneva earlier who had the same date of birth as my mother, but with no matching last name or location.

I had written a letter to every one of those women named Geneva, on January 8, 1998, with no success, but this search was different.

After all these years, I felt hopeful in my heart that this might actually be her. I wanted to call my oldest brother, Jerome, and tell him the news right away, but it was just so hard to believe. I was afraid to become excited until I knew for sure. But, how would I find out for sure?

As I examined the report closer, I noticed an eighty-something-year-old man, with a different last name, living at the same address. It appeared that my mother could be living with an older gentleman. When I searched for the address online, I found the official name of the residence, and it appeared under the category of Nursing Homes. I presumed that my mother was living in a nursing home and that the man in question was a resident in the same nursing home.

Further online research uncovered a phone number to the nursing home. When I called the number, the phone rang several times then gave a busy signal. I called the phone number from late morning until early afternoon and the same thing kept happening. I did some more online research to try to find a phone number to a location nearby, close to the nursing home address.

FINDING MOTHER AFTER FIVE DECADES: A STORY OF HOPE
Grace LaJoy Henderson

I called a nearby nursing facility and spoke with a woman who informed me that the address where my mother appeared to be living was actually a boarding home where numerous people resided.

She told me that the address in question was just one of many boarding homes in the area.

At that point, I called my brother and shared with him my suspicion that I think I may have found our mother, but that I was still trying to figure things out.

My brother asked me what name I had used to find her.

I told him I found her under the current last name she is using and told him the name. I told him I did not want to share all the information with him yet because I was still researching.

Little did I know he took the name I gave him and immediately researched for himself and found the exact same information that I had. Within minutes, he had done an online search for himself then called me back with the same nursing home conclusion that I had come to. He pretty much recounted what had happened to me: a phone that was never picked up.

We both kept trying for hours to call the phone number with hopes someone would eventually answer. Finally, at around seven o'clock that evening, I called the phone number one last time.

This time, a woman actually answered the phone!

FINDING MOTHER AFTER FIVE DECADES: A STORY OF HOPE
Grace LaJoy Henderson

Her name was April. I explained to April that my mother left my five siblings and me with our father when I was only two years old; almost fifty years ago. I told her that I did an online search and it appeared my mother might be living at this boarding home.

She asked what my mother's name was.

I told her the first, middle and last name and asked if there was an older woman with that name living there.

She said there was a Geneva who had my mother's last name, but she did not know her middle name.

I told her my mother's date of birth and asked if it matched the Geneva who lived there.

April confirmed that it was a match!

Still in disbelief, I went on to describe Geneva's skin color. She said my description sounded about right.

When she described Geneva's facial features, my hope increased that this could actually be my mother.

April said it sounded like we were talking about the same Geneva, but she said Geneva never said anything about having children.

"I had always wondered if she had children," April said. "She always acted evasive whenever the subject would come up." She continued, "This all makes sense now."

By this, I think April suspected Geneva's evasiveness may have been a sign of her deep-rooted pain of living so many years

FINDING MOTHER AFTER FIVE DECADES: A STORY OF HOPE
Grace LaJoy Henderson

without her children, or maybe a show of embarrassment for having abandoned us.

Suddenly, April asked me a question that I was not expecting. "Would you like to talk to her?"

I responded, "She can talk!"

You see, I always imagined my mother being immobile, lying in bed at some mental hospital, unable to talk due to being all drugged up. Therefore, when April offered to *go get her* so I could *talk to her* I felt stunned. That was not something I expected to hear at that moment.

April said, "Yes, she can talk," and called her to the phone.

Those few moments of waiting for Geneva to come to the phone felt so surreal. "Am I a really getting ready to hear the voice my own mother after all of these years?" I asked myself.

When Geneva came to the phone she said, "Hello."

Her older, scratchy voice did not sound at all the way I expected. I thought it would sound similar to mine, or my daughter's, or at least similar to one of my sisters'. A part of me really did not think this was the woman I was looking for.

"Hello, is this Geneva?" I said.

I felt my voice trembling, but I strived to maintain my composure.

She said, "Yes."

I told her I believe I may be one of the six children who

FINDING MOTHER AFTER FIVE DECADES: A STORY OF HOPE
Grace LaJoy Henderson

she left in Kansas City almost fifty years ago. I was so nervous that I did not tell her what my name was. I was too busy trying reassure myself of her identity.

I proceeded to ask her some identifying questions.

She answered "yes" to them all in a very calm tone of voice.

Then she asked, "Who is this?"

I felt puzzled about why she asked who I was after she had already answered all of my questions. I felt like if she knew she had abandoned six children, she should have known I was one of them. In hindsight, maybe she needed me to calm down and tell her my name and explain exactly which one of her children I was.

I said, "If all of your responses to my questions are true, then I am your daughter."

She said, "You don't sound like my daughter."

I asked her to confirm her date of birth.

She said, "I'm not answering any more questions because I don't know who you are." She took the phone away from her mouth to talk to April, who was standing beside her while she was talking to me. She said to April, "This doesn't sound like my daughter. This is not my daughter." Then she said to me, "I don't want to talk to you anymore."

April whispered to Geneva, "Ask her to come and see you so you can be sure."

Geneva said, "Come see me."

Those words made me feel very excited and hopeful.

I asked her, "If I came to see you, would you actually talk to me?"

She said, "Yes. Come on," as if she thought I was close by.

I explained to her that she was in a different state and I was in Missouri, so I could not just come right over. But, that I would come as soon as I possibly could. I told her it might be some days or maybe a week or two, but I would definitely be there. I also told her that when I arrive, I would be bringing some of her other children with me. I told her we had all missed her and wanted to see her.

She said, "Okay, come on."

I said, "okay" and asked her to put April back on the phone. I asked April if Geneva actually understood what she was saying to me; and if she was able to understand what I was saying to her.

April assured me that indeed she understood everything I said and that she communicates very well.

"When she has a problem, or if she needs something, she comes to the office and clearly expresses what is on her mind," April said.

I told April that Geneva had confirmed all of the information that I had asked her. I told April I was concerned because I actually asked the questions and Geneva simply replied, "yes" to my questions. She did not actually volunteer any of those facts.

April assured me that Geneva fully understood what she was saying, "yes" to. She told me Geneva was nice and quiet and that she does not bother anybody, she is compliant with taking her medications, she gets up every morning, takes a shower and puts on clean clothes.

"She never has a bad odor like a lot of the other patients who live here," April said. "Her only vice is that she *loves* to smoke! She is in good overall health, except she walks slowly, with a limp, because there is something wrong with her hip."

She also confirmed that my mother has a mental illness.

April continued, "She is fine as long as she takes her medicine. If she were *my* mother, I would bring her to live in my home with me."

She told me how excited she was that I had found my mother, and about the reunion that was soon to take place. She explained that the people who live there do not have families or people who call and come visit them. She told me Geneva had been living there for fifteen years and nobody had ever called or come to visit her.

FINDING MOTHER AFTER FIVE DECADES: A STORY OF HOPE
Grace LaJoy Henderson

She continued, "So when you said you were her daughter, I hurried up and brought her to the phone. We totally support families who are searching for their long-lost loved ones."

April expressed to me that she was very excited about this reunion and that she could not wait. She asked me to be sure to let her know when we were coming so she could make certain she was present for the reunion. She said she did not want to miss this moment. However, she also wanted to be there to support Geneva since this would be a very emotional moment for her.

"I don't want you to think you are coming to some nice place. When you and your brothers see where she is living, you will want to take her up out of here immediately," She said.

She also advised that we probably should not let Geneva know the exact date we were coming because there was a chance she could purposely "run" to avoid meeting us after all of these years.

When I hung up the phone after speaking to my mother and April, I felt a sense of disbelief.

I called my brother, Jerome, and told him I finally got an answer at the phone number that he and I had been dialing all day long. I told him that I actually spoke to our mother! I told him everything she and I had discussed.

FINDING MOTHER AFTER FIVE DECADES: A STORY OF HOPE
Grace LaJoy Henderson

So, when my brother got off the phone with me, he tried calling the phone number one more time and he managed to speak to our mother, too!

He called me back immediately after their talk. His conversation with her was similar to mine. He asked her a few questions about herself to confirm that she was really our mother, and she answered them until finally she insisted that she would not answer any more questions about herself because she did not know who he was.

She ended their conversation by telling him to come see her.

After comparing the details of our conversations, my brother and I felt that we had indeed just found our mother. So, we told our other two brothers and we all became excited about taking a trip to finally meet our long-lost mother for the very first time in almost fifty years!

All of those years of searching finally came to fruition.

The years I almost gave up were overshadowed by the fact I had found my mother!

To learn what happens during the trip, after we arrived, and how our mother reacted when she met us, please read *Reuniting with Mother: A Story of Tenacity*.

FINDING MOTHER AFTER FIVE DECADES: A STORY OF HOPE
Grace LaJoy Henderson

Discussion Questions

1. Name some mental illness behaviors that Mother exhibited before she left her family.

2. Name some ways Father coped with Mother's mental illness. Discuss your response.

3. Growing up, the author felt like Father was the cause of Mother's mental illness becoming more intense. Discuss why you agree or disagree.

4. Do you think it is possible to "knock sense into" a mentally ill person? Why or Why not?

5. Do you think Mother's running away could have been prevented? If so, how? If not, why not?

6. The author specifically remembers being physically harmed by her mother, but still wanted to find her and take care of her. What are your thoughts about that?

FINDING MOTHER AFTER FIVE DECADES: A STORY OF HOPE
Grace LaJoy Henderson

Questions Teachers Can Ask

Critical Thinking/In-depth Comprehension/Writing Skills/Technology Skills

1. What is the main idea or learning experience of the book?

2. Summarize your favorite part of the book and tell why this was your favorite part.

3. Write about an experience in your personal life and tell how it is similar to this story.

4. Write a summary of the story, highlighting what you think the main issues are.

5. To whom would you recommend this book? Why?

6. How can the information in the story be useful in your life or future?

7. Research a famous or infamous person on the computer who was abandoned by their mother, and write a report about that person's life.

8. Research a famous or infamous person on the computer who suffered from a mental illness, and write a report about that person's life.

FINDING MOTHER AFTER FIVE DECADES: A STORY OF HOPE
Grace LaJoy Henderson

Further Discussion Points

Finding Mother after Five Decades indicated some of Geneva's Symptoms and Coping Behaviors for her mental illness. Below are some excerpts from the book that you may use for additional discussion.

Symptoms

Unable to perform Daily Activities. According to the author's father, Geneva was unable to work, cook, clean house, or dress properly. Read and discuss the excerpt below.

I believe my father experienced a lot of stress and disappointment due to my mother having a mental illness and not being able to provide him with the support he desired from a wife. She was unable to work, cook meals, or clean the house the way my father expected her to. **Page 16-17**

Child Abuse. In addition to stories from family members, the author remembers being harmed physically by Geneva. Read and discuss the excerpts below.

I heard stories about my mother's mental illness causing her to experience episodes, which resulted in her harming my siblings and me. **Page 15**

He explained to me that my father usually physically harmed her because she physically harmed us. **Page 15-16**

Then, to come home after a very long, tedious work day and find no dinner ready, the house dirty, or her having harmed one of the children, was an even heavier burden. **Page 17**

Coping Behaviors

Denial. It appears Geneva may have been in denial about having children for all of the years she has been gone. Read and discuss the excerpt below.

April said it sounded like we were talking about the same Geneva, but she said Geneva never said anything about having children. "I had always wondered if she had children," April said. "She always acted evasive whenever the subject would come up." She continued, "This all makes sense now." **Page 64**

These *Further Discussion Points* are only a few things that stood out for the author from her own story. Did you see any additional Symptoms or Coping Behaviors as you read the book? If so, please free to discuss them.

FINDING MOTHER AFTER FIVE DECADES: A STORY OF HOPE
Grace LaJoy Henderson

FINDING MOTHER SERIES

**A Gifted Child in Foster Care:
A Story Resilience – REVISED EDITION**
In this book, Dr. Grace LaJoy shares her life story of being deserted by her mother, living in foster care, and ending up in a gifted and talented class while still in foster care. She recalls her life story before, during and after foster care. The *Finding Mother Series* was written as a sequel to this book.

**Finding Mother After Five Decades:
A Story of Hope**
Grace LaJoy's determination pays off when she finally finds her mother who abandoned her at age two. Discover the specific details about her intriguing journey in **Finding Mother after Five Decades,** BOOK 1 of the *Finding Mother Series.*

**Reuniting with Mother:
A Story of Tenacity**
What happens when Grace LaJoy and her siblings come face-to-face with their estranged mother after 49 years? How does she receive them? Find out in **Reuniting with Mother,** BOOK 2 of the *Finding Mother Series.*

FINDING MOTHER AFTER FIVE DECADES: A STORY OF HOPE
Grace LaJoy Henderson

**After the Reunion:
A Story of Acceptance**
After a very emotional reunion, Grace LaJoy has two concerns to address with her long-lost mother. What are her concerns? Does she get the answers she needs from her mother? Find out in **After the Reunion,** BOOK 3 of the *Finding Mother Series.*

**Diary of Emotion:
Thoughts and Feelings**
After reuniting with her mother after 49 years, Grace LaJoy toils with an array of thoughts and feeling. She reveals them all in **Diary of Emotions,** BOOK 4 of the *Finding Mother Series.*

Available in softcover and Kindle eBook
Collect them all at Amazon.com
Ask for the series in
bookstores and libraries
www.gracelajoy.com

FINDING MOTHER AFTER FIVE DECADES: A STORY OF HOPE
Grace LaJoy Henderson

PRAISES FOR THE FINDING MOTHER SERIES

Grace LaJoy Henderson's *Finding Mother Series* is a revelation. It is a gift to discover an author who can write so honestly—and with such vulnerability—about the joy and pain of reuniting with a parent after a 49-year separation. Henderson never glosses over the frightening or disappointing parts of her story. But her compassionate, unwavering voice, as she uncovers the long arc of her mother's life, is itself a triumph. **~Whitney Terrell, Associate Professor of English, University of Missouri-Kansas City**

"The author's emotional honesty and the balancing of positive and negative emotions is what makes this series work." **~Phoebe Shanahan, MA in English Literature**

"The Finding Mother Series will inspire readers to *feel* their feelings. It stirs people in similar situations to be at peace, but at the same time seek growth, in the midst of their circumstances." **Arica Miller, LMSW, School Social Worker**

"The *Finding Mother Series* displays a perfect example of how one triggering event can cause conflicting emotions. Throughout the series, the author experienced hope *and* despair, excitement *and* apprehension. Two, totally opposite emotions both at the same time. However, both were completely justified! This range and transition of emotions is what drives the entire *series*. Secondary students will absolutely benefit from reading this collection of books." **~Jacob Kelow, M.S.Ed., Secondary School Counselor, Kansas City Public Schools**

PRAISES continued →

FINDING MOTHER AFTER FIVE DECADES: A STORY OF HOPE
Grace LaJoy Henderson

"The *Finding Mother Series* is written in a very powerful, real and authentic voice style. The author's honesty shines through her writing. Although the author's sadness throughout the story is quite palpable, her attitude towards her mentally ill mother is full of grace and understanding despite the fact that she had abandoned her. This is a clear and honest work." ~**Fay Collins, Writer-Editor**

"The *Finding Mother Series* is a beautiful sequence of books. The author's reunion with her mother is very well documented." ~**Phyllis Harris, Former Missouri State Director, Parent Information Resource Center**

"The author shares her personal story in an authentic way. Easy reading. Flows well." ~**Ila Barrett, Behavioral Therapist, Jacksonville, FL**

"The Finding Mother Series is an inspiration to all who have faced abandonment by a parent. Grace LaJoy's truth validates her determination never to extinguish the fire, which burned in her soul to find her mother." ~ **Dr. Gwendolyn Squires, Former School Principal, Kansas City Public Schools**

"Reading this series may help others who long to be reunited with their parents." ~**Dr. Mary E. McConnell, Educator, University of Missouri-Kansas City**

"The Finding Mother Series will touch many people who are in this same situation, but who may not have the forgiveness in their hearts that the author and her siblings have. It is going to touch lives in more ways than you can imagine." ~**Jean Smith, Dallas, TX**

"I strongly believe that this series will heal a lot of broken hearts and act as a source of encourage, advice, guidance and counsel for people in such scenarios; both children and adults." ~**Ken J.**

FINDING MOTHER AFTER FIVE DECADES: A STORY OF HOPE
Grace LaJoy Henderson

About the Author

Dr. Grace LaJoy Henderson is the author of over thirty books. Her foster care story, *A Gifted Child in Foster Care: A Story of Resilience, Classroom Set* and her children's book series, *The Gracie Series*, are currently being used in public and charter schools.

Pearson Higher Education published two chapters from her foster care story in a college textbook.

She has earned a Doctorate in Christian Counseling, a Master's of Education in Guidance and Counseling, and a Master of Arts in Curriculum and Instruction. She has also earned a Bachelor's degree in Social Psychology.

Dr. Henderson managed a contract with the Missouri Children's Division, in which she provided court ordered mentoring for foster youth, supervised parent-child visits and parent education. She has served as psychology and college success instructor as well as academic coach. Outside of higher education, she is a keynote speaker, workshop leader and guest author at schools, libraries and other organizations. Newspapers, radio and television has featured her publications and her story.

FINDING MOTHER AFTER FIVE DECADES: A STORY OF HOPE
Grace LaJoy Henderson

www.ingramcontent.com/pod-product-compliance
Lightning Source LLC
Chambersburg PA
CBHW052113070526
44584CB00017B/2466